I hope you get a pug
one day!
— Eliana

PUG MUGS:
JUVENILE DELINQUENTS

PUG MUGS:
JUVENILE DELINQUENTS

WILLOW CREEK PRESS®

Published by Willow Creek Press, Inc.
P.O. Box 147, Minocqua, Wisconsin 54548

Design: Donnie Rubo
Printed in China

NAME: MAX
HEIGHT: 10"
WEIGHT: 8 LBS.

CHARGE: FAILURE TO YIELD
Infraction

The four natural laws of retrieving require that a canine (1) chase after a ball thrown by its master; (2) secure said ball in its mouth; (3) return to its master, and (4) yield the ball to said master's hand. Max has consistently ignored rules (3) and (4) by possessively running around the yard with no apparent intention to yield. A repeat offender, Max has been deemed an incorrigible case with no further charges pending.

NAME: BUSTER
HEIGHT: 14"
WEIGHT: 12 LBS.

CHARGE: BURGLARY
Felony

Already a known felon and naughty puppy, Buster illegally nosed open the kitchen closet door and tore open a bag of doggy snacks. He was not apprehended until half the bag had been eaten and regurgitated upon the floor. As a result of this serious incident security has been tightened throughout the household.

NAME: TOBY
HEIGHT: 8"
WEIGHT: 6 LBS.

CHARGE: VICIOUS GOSSIPING
Misdemeanor

Although professional trainers were hired to mold
Toby into an aggressive guard dog, his mild-mannered
nature proved incompatible with the job description.
His owners are encouraged however that Toby has at
least demonstrated that he can be a vicious gossip.
He has been sentenced to six weeks of further
training.

NAME: TEDDY
HEIGHT: 13"
WEIGHT: 13 LBS.

CHARGE: HIDING A KNOWN FELON
Felony

Authorities, in search of a naughty neighborhood runaway Yorkie identified as Coco, were initially barred entry to Teddy's doghouse. The standoff continued until Teddy was tempted from the doorstep by a Scooby snack, after which an official accessed the house and discovered Coco huddled in a corner.

NAME: MAGGIE
HEIGHT: 7"
WEIGHT: 5 LBS.

CHARGE: **IMPERSONATING A SERVICE DOG**
Misdemeanor

In order to fly first class with her master, Maggie attempted to pass airline security representing herself as a service dog. Alert TSA officials, doubting the dog had completed the required training at such a tender age, demanded credentials. Unable to provide the documentation, Maggie was placed behind bars in a kennel cage and condemned to fly in the baggage hold to Los Angeles.

NAME: BEAR
HEIGHT: 11"
WEIGHT: 10 LBS.

CHARGE: TAMPERING WITH EVIDENCE
Misdemeanor

Turning in rapid circles at the door, Bear anxiously
signaled his need to perform his outside duty.
Immediately after his release the desperate pug
relieved himself in the flower garden rather than
upon the lawn. Aware of the seriousness of his
transgression, Bear chose to ingest and eliminate
the evidence. His crime came at the cost of severe
stomach cramps. Sentence was reduced to time served.

NAME: ROSIE
HEIGHT: 14"
WEIGHT: 11 LBS.

CHARGE: **BACKSEAT DRIVING AND OBSTRUCTING A DRIVER'S VIEW**

Infraction

Rosie's insistence on leaning out of the backseat window of the Winkler's vehicle resulted in an obstructed view through the rearview mirror. Authorities responded to this dangerous situation by rolling up the window. Case closed.

NAME: SAMMY
HEIGHT: 13"
WEIGHT: 10 LBS.

CHARGE: ELOPING WITH A MINOR
Felony

Sammy and Willow are neighbors who apparently
developed an unusual fondness for one another. On
the afternoon of July 17th their owners noted that
both pugs went missing and an immediate search was
undertaken. The dogs were soon discovered in the
park before an apparent romantic tryst could be
consummated. Because Willow is only nine months old,
charges were originally filed against Sammy until
a brief investigation revealed that Sammy himself
is one month younger. Confused officials dropped all
charges, but suggested that the amorous pugs be
closely supervised in the future.

NAME: ZOE
HEIGHT: 11"
WEIGHT: 9 LBS.

CHARGE: COMPUTER CRIME
Felony

Dick and Kathy Anderson were temporarily unaware of the following email from the veterinary clinic: "Your dog Zoe is due for her annual visit. Please call to schedule an appointment. Thank you." It is undetermined how the message was deleted, but the Anderson's have their suspicions. The email was ultimately discovered in the "Trash" file in time for Zoe's sentencing to the clinic.

NAME: DUKE
HEIGHT: 9"
WEIGHT: 7 LBS.

CHARGE: BREAKING AND ENTERING
Felony

Duke's owners opted for a brief swim in the lake to work up an appetite before enjoying their summer picnic lunch. Unfortunately, they did not factor in the nefarious scheme their pug had quickly hatched. Wasting no time, Duke broke into the picnic basket and devoured two BLTs, potato chips, pickles, and an undetermined number of cookies before his apprehension. He was imprisoned in the vehicle for the remainder of the picnic.

NAME: DAISY
HEIGHT: 11"
WEIGHT: 8 LBS.

CHARGE: RECKLESS ENDANGERMENT
Infraction

Channeling her inner Labrador retriever, Daisy
attempted to fetch a ball tossed into the family
pool. Within one minute authorities themselves
entered the pool to fetch the exhausted pug.

NAME: OLIVER
HEIGHT: 12"
WEIGHT: 11 LBS.

CHARGE: **DESTRUCTION OF EVIDENCE**
Misdemeanor

"Don't fall for that innocent look, he knows darn
well that he did it", stated Deborah Morgan in
her damning testimony against Oliver. "One minute
that last slice of Cracker Barrel cheddar was right
there on the picnic table and the next it was gone."
Verdict is pending.

NAME: LUCKY
HEIGHT: 9"
WEIGHT: 6 LBS.

CHARGE: LEWD AND LACIVIOUS BEHAVIOR

Misdemeanor

Authorities are baffled by Lucky whose vulgar, suggestive gestures directed toward female dogs at the local dog park have many owners upset. "I just don't get it," said one of the investigators on the scene, "the little guy is only six months, old but acts like a professional stud."

NAME: LOLA
HEIGHT: 8"
WEIGHT: 6 LBS.

CHARGE: ATTEMPTED HOMICIDE
Felony

"I don't know what she rolled in, but the stink
brought me to my knees," testified Barbara Kramer
at an initial hearing involving the family pug, Lola,
who returned home after an unauthorized tour of
the neighborhood. "My clothes reeked. My eyes were
bleeding. I thought I was going to die." Ms. Kramer
survived the incident.

NAME: OSCAR
HEIGHT: 14"
WEIGHT: 12 LBS.

CHARGE: ILLEGAL BORDER CROSSING
Felony

Pookie, the Shi Tzu living next door to Oscar, remains on high alert after the pug puppy's audacious raid into her backyard, where he ran across her grass and grabbed her stick before she could chase him back across her backyard with her stick to his own property. The crime remains under investigation.

NAME: GINGER
HEIGHT: 6"
WEIGHT: 4 LBS.

CHARGE: SUSPICIOUS BEHAVIOR
Charges pending

After the disappearance of the candy canes hanging on the lowest tier of Terry and Jessie Schulz's Christmas tree, suspicion has fallen upon Ginger. "We can't prove she did it," said Jessie, "but you can see that she just looks guilty." Ginger remains under heavy surveillance through the Holiday season.

NAME: COOPER
HEIGHT: 11"
WEIGHT: 8 LBS.

CHARGE: PETTY LARCENY
Misdemeanor

A cookie slipped from the hand of six-year-old Halle
Morgan and fell to the kitchen floor where Cooper
immediately seized and swallowed it. A distraught
Halle sobbed at her loss as Cooper begged for more.
Charges were dismissed after Halle was
given another cookie.

NAME: BELLE
HEIGHT: 8"
WEIGHT: 6 LBS.

CHARGE: DOMESTIC DISTURBANCE
Misdemeanor

Authorities Bill and Joyce responded to a loud
backyard disturbance and found their pugs, two-
year-old Harlow and six-month-old Belle, in a heated
scuffle over possession of a chew stick. Each dog
was seized by the collar and a brief interrogation
ensued. Interviews failed to establish a perpetrator
and both dogs were soon released with a warning.

NAME: LOU
HEIGHT: 11"
WEIGHT: 11 LBS.

CHARGE: CRIMINAL TRESPASS
Felony

It is understood that access to the overstuffed,
green leather chair in the living room is strictly
limited to Ryan, the master of the house. When
evidence in the form of tan-colored fur was
discovered upon this chair, investigators associated
it with Lou, the family pug. A home security camera
directed toward the chair ultimately caught the
suspect in the act.

NAME: MURPHY

HEIGHT: 13"

WEIGHT: 15 LBS.

CHARGE: **WANTON AND WILLFUL FLATULENCE**

Misdemeanor

On August 14th, as the Olson's entertained company on their outside deck, Murphy was observed lying on his side emitting frightful sounds and odors. The continuous cocophony prompted Jake Olson to publicly apologize for the gaseous pug's behavior. "This is no accident," noted one of the guests. "Look at him, he's staring right at us and doing it on purpose." Murphy was sentenced to the garage for the remainder of the evening.

NAME: FELIX
HEIGHT: 14"
WEIGHT: 12 LBS.

CHARGE: GANG LEADER
Felony

Although the youngest and smallest dog in the pack,
Felix has managed to work his way up to gang leader
through dint of courage and an uncanny ability to
turn over garbage cans. His elusiveness at being
caught-in-the-act confounds authorities, but he
remains under surveillance.

NAME: CHICO
HEIGHT: 10"
WEIGHT: 9 LBS.

CHARGE: ILLEGAL IMMIGRATION
Felony

Chico escaped a shelter home for dogs in Juarez and
crossed the Rio Grande in broad daylight to reach
the U.S. border literally under the noses of Border
Patrol agents. To pursue a better life he is believed
to have worked at odd jobs across the country and,
although his whereabouts are unknown, authorities
are currently acting on a tip that he is part of a
sled dog team outside of Nome.

NAME: BILLY
HEIGHT: 8"
WEIGHT: 7 LBS.

CHARGE: **DAMAGE TO A MOTOR VEHICLE**
Felony

Willy and Billy, a pair of six-month-old pugs,
were confined together in a Dodge Caravan for
approximately one-half an hour. Ms. Alisa Bensen,
owner of the vehicle, reports that she returned to
find serious damage to the leather steering wheel as
the apparent result of gnawing. After questioning,
neither pup could be proved culpable and no charges
were filed.

NAME: BOONE
HEIGHT: 7"
WEIGHT: 4 LBS.

CHARGE: **THREATENING A WITNESS**
Felony

After his littermate observed him chewing
on a forbidden child's toy, Boone shot him an
unmistakable, threatening look intended to silence
any future testimony against him. Boone remains
free.

NAME: LEO
HEIGHT: 10"
WEIGHT: 12 LBS.

CHARGE: AUTOMOBILE ACCIDENT
Felony

Left unattended in the family Lexus while his
owners Tim and Barb shopped at the local Target
store, an uncomfortable Leo mistook the release
of an intestinal gas bubble for something far
more serious and substantive. Because the accident
occurred in the driver's seat charges were increased
from misdemeanor to felony level.

NAME: BUBBA
HEIGHT: 9"
WEIGHT: 10 LBS.

CHARGE: **PUBLIC CORRUPTION**
Felony

On May 25th Bubba did willfully and with malice
aforethought commit public corruption at and on
the public square. He remained unrepentant as his
master, with considerable embarrassment, bagged the
evidence.

NAME: LEVI
HEIGHT: 11"
WEIGHT: 12 LBS.

CHARGE: GROSS NEGLIGENCE
Misdemeanor

Original charges of willful disobedience were
reduced to gross negligence after the following
testimony from owner Amy: "It's not so much that
he's disobeying, it's more like he's just lying there
ignoring me. He just doesn't seem to care about
anything but napping and eating."

NAME: TINA
HEIGHT: 12"
WEIGHT: 13 LBS.

CHARGE: SPEEDING IN A SCHOOL ZONE
Misdemeanor

Tina repeatedly ignored prominently displayed
cautionary street signs to pursue her new-found
passion for speed skateboarding. Exasperated
officials were ultimately inclined to confiscate
the vehicle and sentence Tina to home confinement
during school hours.

NAME: EDDY
HEIGHT: 9"
WEIGHT: 9 LBS.

CHARGE: **BAIL JUMPING**
Felony

After continually demonstrating an unwillingness
to stay in his own yard, Eddy was imprisoned in the
kennel cage for punishment. After a one hour time-
out a seemingly repentant Eddy was released outside
on his own recognizance and took the opportunity to
immediately flee the yard. He is still at large.

NAME: HEMI
HEIGHT: 10"
WEIGHT: 12 LBS.

CHARGE: WILLFUL DISOBEDIENCE
Misdemeanor

Noted dog psychic Carlos Ramone observed a video
of Hemi's behavior at the beach and channeled
this stream of consciousness: "Hemi is literally
saying to himself, 'No way, no way, no way. I'm not
going anywhere. Pull on that stupid leash all you
want you putz, but I'm staying right here.'" Based
largely on Ramone's expert testimony, Hemi has been
prohibited from further seaside visits.

NAME: SAM
HEIGHT: 9"
WEIGHT: 11 LBS.

CHARGE: FELONIOUS FINICKINESS
Felony

Sam has been charged with chronic consumption of myriad junk/snack foods leading to a stubborn disinterest in the nutritious dog food offered to him twice daily. "He just stares at his regular kibbles," a concerned owner testified, "but hardly ever eats them. Maybe he'll push them around with his nose a little. That's about it." A 30-day dietary rehabilitation is expected to lead to serious interim withdrawal, but ultimate full recovery.

NAME: BOO
HEIGHT: 7"
WEIGHT: 5 LBS.

CHARGE: COERCION
Misdemeanor

Boo is a scheming little puppy, so confident in his
cuteness that he regularly and willfully succeeds
in coercing tickles and belly rubs from unsuspecting
owners Carl and Esther Woodman who have been named
as accomplices in the ongoing investigation.

NAME: KIBBLE
HEIGHT: 13"
WEIGHT: 13 LBS.

CHARGE: **DESTRUCTION OF PRIVATE PROPERTY**

Misdemeanor

Kibble has been a frequent trespasser in George Trimble's yard where he is so fond of relieving himself on a particular azalea that he has caused its gradual and ultimate destruction. Trimble is filing charges against Kibble's owners.

NAME: HUNTER
HEIGHT: 12"
WEIGHT: 15 LBS.

CHARGE: FUGITIVE FLIGHT
Misdemeanor

Sure enough, no sooner did Claire release Hunter
from his leash that he sped headlong down the
beach. Ignoring calls for him to return to heel
he flushed several flocks of terns and sandpipers
before rolling in a dead mullet. Finally subdued and
returned to leash, Hunter was subjected to a stern
rebuke.

NAME: DRAKE
HEIGHT: 9"
WEIGHT: 11 LBS.

CHARGE: MAYHEM
Felony

What began as innocent cuddling of the family cat escalated to violence when Drake forbid said cat to slip from his clutches. "It all started out friendly and cute," testified a witness, "but things kind of got out of hand when Drake went from hugging to pawing to all-out wrestling." As the incident resulted in no serious injuries charges were dropped.

NAME: WINSTON
HEIGHT: 8"
WEIGHT: 9 LBS.

CHARGE: CRIMINAL INTENT
Misdemeanor

Drawn to the aroma of fresh-baked cutout cookies,
Winston surreptitiously entered the kitchen and
managed, despite his diminutive stature, to scale
a stool to elevate himself to the counter. While
pausing to consider the risk-reward scenario, his
master entered the kitchen. A startled Winston fled
the scene. The ensuing investigation determined that,
although the alleged perp did not in fact eat a
cookie, drops of saliva found upon the counter are
key elements in the prosecution's case.

NAME: JUNIPER
HEIGHT: 8"
WEIGHT: 6 LBS.

CHARGE: **VOYEURISM**
Misdemeanor

Authorities responded to a complaint at 714 Beaumont Avenue involving a six-month-old pug identified as Juniper who was observed at her backyard fence wantonly staring at a rib roast as it was carved on the neighbor's picnic table. Subject was incarcerated within the confines of her home.

NAME: MARTIN
HEIGHT: 6"
WEIGHT: 5 LBS.

CHARGE: ESCAPE
Felony

Martin's owners were confident that the metal
fence enclosing their backyard was sufficient
to hold him. This confidence lead to a degree of
complacency sufficient enough to allow Martin, over
an undetermined period of time, to dig a hole under
the fence through which he escaped last Friday.
Authorities have posted an APB to the neighborhood
and Martin's capture is deemed imminent.

NAME: BELLA
HEIGHT: 7"
WEIGHT: 7 LBS.

CHARGE: VANDALISM

Misdemeanor

Caught in the act of gnawing on the wooden leg of a
footstool, Bella was given a stern verbal reprimand.
Her obvious remorse over the incident broke the
hearts of officials and no further charges were
filed.

NAME: BOBO
HEIGHT: 10"
WEIGHT: 11 LBS.

CHARGE: EXCESSIVE REMORSE
Infraction

"He acted like I spanked him or something," testified
Susan Carlson in the case of Bobo vs. Carlson. "Talk
about overacting with all that whimpering and
crying. Honestly, all I said was 'no' when he tried to
jump on the chair."

NAME: SIMBA
HEIGHT: 11"
WEIGHT: 13 LBS.

CHARGE: GRAFFITI
Misdemeanor

Several times daily Simba is allowed outside to
relieve himself. His owners were recently shocked to
discover that what was once perceived as a normal
piddling routine was revealed in fact as a self-
indulgent, vandalous act of graffiti when it was
determined that the yellow spots on the lawn formed
the capital letter "S".

NAME: SCOUT
HEIGHT: 10"
WEIGHT: 12 LBS.

CHARGE: **FAILURE TO REPORT AN ACCIDENT**

Misdemeanor

A puddle of piddle discovered on the Smith's hardwood living room floor could be attributed only to Scout, the sole pet occupying the home. When confronted with the evidence Scout assumed an air of surprise and bewilderment as to the cause of the accident.

NAME: PUGGIE
HEIGHT: 8"
WEIGHT: 10 LBS.

CHARGE: **COWARDICE IN THE FACE OF THE ENEMY**

Felony

Francis, the eight-year-old family cat, has been sullen since the surprise appearance of Puggie, the new pug puppy, in the household she once considered her personal domain. Puggie has repeatedly offered friendly overtures to Francis only to be rebuffed with hisses and scratching claws. A frightened but eternally optimistic Puggie has resigned himself to the backseat in the pet hierarchy and has been branded a coward.

NAME: BONES
HEIGHT: 12"
WEIGHT: 12 LBS.

CHARGE: STOWAWAY
Infraction

Deducing by the unusual activity in the household
that his family was preparing for vacation without
him, Bones cleverly concealed himself within the
luggage. This desperate ploy was soon discovered and
a glum Bones was sentenced to 10 days at Sunshine
Kennels.